The Last Abbot of Wymondham

Wymondham Abbey Seal

Mary and Terry Miller

© T. E. & M. Miller 2004

First published 2004

All rights reserved. No part of this publication may be reproduced, in any form or by any means, without the prior consent of the authors.

ISBN 0 900616 72 5

Printed and published by
Geo. R. Reeve Ltd., 9-11 Town Green, Wymondham, Norfolk, NR18 0BD.

Foreword

This scholarly document will be a joy to read for anyone who is interested in the history of five hundred years ago and more especially where it relates to Norfolk.

Considerable research has been undertaken to produce the detailed facts about the last Abbot of Wymondham. The genealogy is fascinating, bringing the history up to date by showing that one of the successors of Loye Ferrers was the subject matter of a 1940's film, "The Wicked Lady," in which Margaret Lockwood starred.

A short booklet, well written and, although full of facts, easily assimilated. I wish the reader pleasure.

The Rt. Hon: The Earl Ferrers

Part of the probate copy of the will of Loye Ferrers, 1548.

Crown copyright.

The monastery at Wymondham

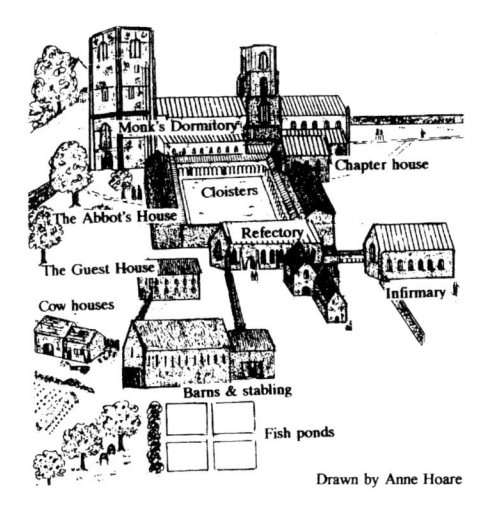

Drawn by Anne Hoare

The monastery at Wymondham was founded in 1107 as a cell of the Benedictine Abbey of St. Albans by William d'Albini whose brother Richard was Abbot of St. Albans from 1097-1119. William d'Albini of Buckenham castle was chief butler to Henry I and had earlier been granted the Manor of Wymondham by William the Conqueror.

The Benedictine or Black monks wore a habit of a black cowl and a black tunic girded with a leather belt. They followed the Rule of St. Benedict and practised moderation, prudence and a humane conception of monasticism.

The monasteries were self sufficient and independent. The monks, who came from various social backgrounds and were of

A Benedictine monk

varied age, were mostly unordained. There were both educated priests and illiterate lay brothers. Monks were often sent to Oxford or Cambridge University to take degrees and some remained there as scholars.

Initially the monastery at Wymondham would have consisted of a Prior and around twelve monks. To support the monastery d'Albini endowed it with several estates and one third of the Manor of Wymondham. In 1448, the Priory was elevated to Abbey status and became independent of St. Albans; although, undoubtedly, close links were retained. From that time the monks were granted the right to elect their own Abbot.

A sixteenth century Abbot

The Abbots of Wymondham

1448 Stephen London

1466 William Bokenham

1471 John Kertelyng

1502 John Redmayne

1511 Thomas Chandler

1514 Thomas Chamberlain

1517 John Bransforth

1520 John Lord Bishop of Lechlin

1526 William Castleton

1532 Loye (Eligius) Ferrers

The Rule of St. Benedict established the name Abbot as the superior of an independent monastery. Abbeys were autonomous and the Abbot, who was a member of the local political elite, had unlimited power, but he had to listen to the counsel of his senior monks. If he was granted episcopal exemption, he was answerable only to the Pope and did not have to heed the Bishop or Archbishop. At Henry VIII's dissolution of the monasteries in 1538, the then and last Abbot of Wymondham was Loye or Eligius Ferrers.

The Ferrers family

Loye Ferrers was a descendant of the de Ferrers family which came to England with the Norman invasion. Loye's branch of the family stems from William de Ferrers, Lord of Groby, a title gifted in the thirteenth century by his mother Margaret the wife of William de Ferrers of Derby and the eldest daughter of Roger de Quincy, Earl of Winchester and Lord Groby. This branch of the family thereafter bore the de Quincy arms (gulles, seven voided lozenges or conjoined, three, three and one), instead of the original de Ferrers arms (argent, six horseshoes sable pierced or, three, two and one). In the early fifteenth century some members of the family settled in St. Albans. Unfortunately, the precise relationships within Loye's generation and the immediately preceding generations is somewhat uncertain. The pedigree shows the best estimate of the lineage from the available evidence, including earlier published pedigrees. Some earlier authors have suggested that Loye was the uncle of George Ferrers. This probably arose from the fact that there was thirty years between the death of Loye and that of George. However, from Loye's last will and testament it is clear that George was his brother. They may in

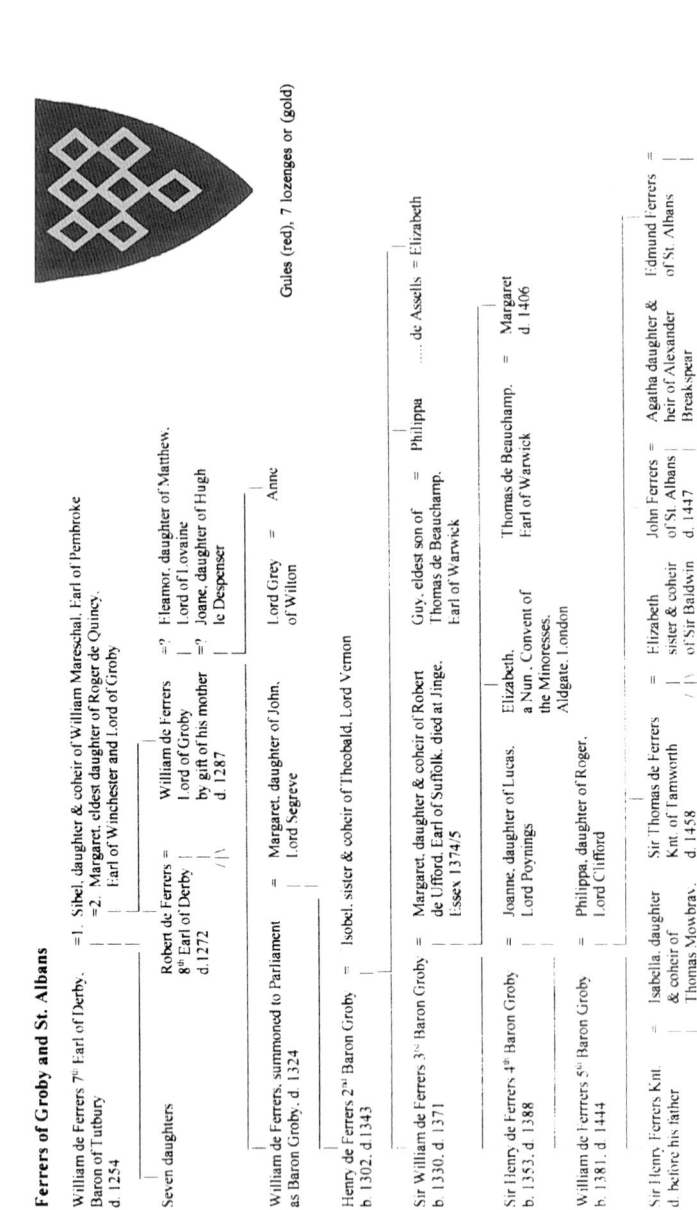

Ferrers of Groby and St. Albans

Gules (red), 7 lozenges or (gold)

William de Ferrers 7th Earl of Derby, Baron of Tutbury d. 1254
= 1. Sibel, daughter & coheir of William Mareschal, Earl of Pembroke
= 2. Margaret, eldest daughter of Roger de Quincy, Earl of Winchester and Lord of Groby

Seven daughters

Robert de Ferrers 8th Earl of Derby, d.1272 =

William de Ferrers Lord of Groby by gift of his mother d. 1287 =? Eleanor, daughter of Matthew, Lord of Lovaine =? Joane, daughter of Hugh le Despenser

William de Ferrers, summoned to Parliament as Baron Groby, d. 1324 = Margaret, daughter of John, Lord Segreve

Lord Grey of Wilton = Anne

Henry de Ferrers 2nd Baron Groby, b 1302, d 1343 = Isobel, sister & coheir of Theobald, Lord Vernon

Sir William de Ferrers 3rd Baron Groby, b 1330, d. 1371 = Margaret, daughter & coheir of Robert de Ufford, Earl of Suffolk, died at Jinge, Essex 1374/5

Guy, eldest son of Thomas de Beauchamp, Earl of Warwick = Philippa ...... de Assells = Elizabeth

Sir Henry de Ferrers 4th Baron Groby, b. 1353, d. 1388 = Joanne, daughter of Lucas, Lord Poynings

Elizabeth, a Nun. Convent of the Minoresses, Aldgate, London

Thomas de Beauchamp, Earl of Warwick = Margaret d. 1406

William de Ferrers 5th Baron Groby, b. 1381, d. 1444 = Philippa, daughter of Roger, Lord Clifford

Sir Henry Ferrers Knt d. before his father = Isabella, daughter & coheir of Thomas Mowbray, Duke of Norfolk

Sir Thomas de Ferrers Knt. of Tamworth d. 1458

Elizabeth, sister & coheir of Sir Baldwin Freville = John Ferrers of St. Albans d. 1447 = Agatha daughter & heir of Alexander Breakspear

Edmund Ferrers of St. Albans = ___ ___ c

a   b

4

Ferrers Family Tree

```
a ─────────────────────────────────────────────────── b ─────────── c

Sir Edward Grey = Elizabeth        John Ferrers = Catherine, sister & heir of Sir Edward Benstede
                  heiress of Groby              │  of Bennington, Herts.
                                   d. 1488      │
                                                │
  ┌──────────┬─────────────┬──────┐             ├─────────────────────────────┬─────── Alice
  │          │             │      │             │                             │
Edward     William      William  Grace      Thomas Ferrers  =1. Alice, daughter of
Ferrers    Ferrers      Victor              of St. Albans      John Cockworthy of Devon
d. 1468                 d. 1486/7            d. 1534         =2. Margaret ......
                                                                ?
  ┌──────────────────┐
  │                  │
John Ferrers     Loye Ferrers              George Ferrers of Markyate  =1. Elizabeth, widow of        Jane         daughter
d. before 1534   Abbot of Wymondham.        b. 1512. d. Flamsted 1578      Humphrey Boucher, m. 1541, d. 1546
                 Archdeacon of Suffolk.                                 =2. Jane Southcote. m 1546
                 d. 1548                                                =3. Margaret Preston . m 1569

                     ┌──────┬──────┐
                     │      │      │
                    Mary   Jane   Julius Ferrers of Markyate   =   Susan,
                                  d. Flamsted 1596                 daughter of Sir John Boteler Knt.
                                                                   of Watton Woodhall, Herts

Sir John Ferrers Knt  =1. Anne daughter of Sir George Knighton Knt. of Bayford, Kent
of Punsborne              b. 1586. m. 1604, d. 1630
b 1575, d. 1640       =2. Elizabeth daughter of Sir Edmund Lucy Knt of Broxbourne, Herts.

Knighton Ferrers esq  =   Katherine                         ┌──────┬──────┬──────┬──────┬──────┬──────┐
b 1603, d. 1640           daughter & coheir of Sir William  John   Julius John   Henry  Charles George Katherine
                          Walter Knt. of Wimbledon          b. 1609 b.1612 b.1614 b.1615 b.1618 b.1621 b.1610/11
                          [= Sir Simon Fanshawe Knt.]       d. 1610 d.1613 d.1615 d.1623 d.1627

Thomas Fanshawe       =   Katherine Ferrers          ┌──────────┬──────────┬──────────┐
succeeded his father      'The Wicked Lady of Markyate'  John    Knighton   Elizabeth
as Viscount Fanshawe      b. 1633. m. 1646. d. 1660     d. 1639  b. & d. 1639  d. 1633
1665, d 1674
```

previously been let but the parsonage was leased to Miss Litellprowe and Henry Fuller, alderman of Norwich, by indenture for 15 years. The letter was signed by Abbot Loye Ferrers, Thomas Thaxted, cellarer, Thomas Lynne, subprior, John Harlyston, third prior, Richard Chambryge, sub-chanter, Edward Saham, precentor, Robert Colchester, sexton, John Wyndham, John Hoxton and Robert Westwood. A second letter followed on 13th September giving details of previous arrangements and apparently not agreeing to the lease as the monks would then have to sell their sheep and buy mutton in the market.

Thomas Cromwell

Like his predecessor, William Castleton, he was astute enough to recognize the way the political wind was blowing. Four years before the dissolution of the monasteries, he and ten monks subscribed to the Royal Supremacy, as did Prior Castleton and the monks of Norwich. At the Dissolution, the last corporate act of the monastery was to grant him the vicarage of Wymondham. He was also assigned a pension of £60 13s. 0d. per annum. Interestingly, in 1555, several years after Loye's death, his brother George was still receiving an annuity of 40 shillings from the monastery. Loye kept on the right side of John Flowerdew, Sergeant-at-law, who had been appointed by the commissioners to supervise the pulling down of the monastery, by leasing him his residence at Downham, Wymondham.

Loye Ferrers the cleric

On the 20th October 1538 Loye received dispensation to hold a benefice and change habit, thereby allowing him to make the change from a regular priest to a secular cleric. On February 7th 1539, he was created a Doctor of Theology by Thomas Cranmer, Archbishop of Canterbury. He only remained vicar of Wymondham for one year. In 1539, on the retirement of his friend William Castleton, who at the Dissolution had become the first Dean of Norwich Cathedral, he was appointed to the office of Sixth Prebend of the Cathedral, replacing John Salisbury who became the new Dean. The Sixth Prebend (the Prebend of Yarmouth) was supported by the income of the former monastery at Yarmouth. Dean Castleton is recorded as having found appointments for several of his former monks. The Cathedral was expected to provide prebendaries with a house in the cathedral close. However, even by 1610 accommodation had only been found for three prebends. It is therefore most likely that Loye would have purchased a property of his own in Norwich. On the 8th

A sixteenth century cleric

February 1542 Loye was also created Archdeacon of Suffolk, a post he held until his death in 1548.

The last will and testament of Loye Ferrers, which was made 24th February 1547/8 and proved in London, 21st November 1548, provides a belated insight into his character. He appears to have been a compassionate, generous and meticulous man with close ties to his family. As would have been expected for a man of his calling, he left money to the Cathedral at Norwich. He also left money for the maintenance of the Church of Great Yarmouth and to the poor of that town. He bequeathed *"to Sr. William Stone priest of Bungay for the gratefulness he found in him a copull of lynge and three copull of coddes and in money twenty shillings."* Following the Dissolution, many monks found positions as chantry priests, and like vicars of the time would have been titled Sr. (Sir). Mr. Castleton priest of Norwich received four pairs of lyng and six pairs of cod. The fish, lyng and cod, were presumably supplied as part of the income of the Prebend of Yarmouth. He must have had close links with Bungay as Mr. Parsons and Sr. Warton from there both received gold rings. Sr. Robert Berry sometime monk of Wymondham received 6s. 8d. as did two other monks, and Sr. Essex one of his executors got £6 and his *"best furred gown with tenne such books as he shall thinke most mete for his purpose."* Other friends and servants received generous bequests. He bequeathed to a friend from Yarmouth, *"for his gentleness and paynes taken for me at London,"* 40 shillings and to the friend's daughter, his godchild, 20 shillings. His past and present servants, cooks and housekeeper all received legacies. Moreover, he requested that his current servants should be employed by his cousin John Butler for one year after his death.

Loye Ferrers also seems to have retained a connection with his family in his native Hertfordshire. He loaned his brother's wife Elizabeth £80 to pay part of her deceased first husband's debts. Her first husband, Sir Humphrey Bourchier, died with debts of over £1000 but was also owed money; particularly £200 by Sir Francis Bryan. Consequently, George and Elizabeth Ferrers applied to the Court of Requests with a Bill of Complaint against Sir Francis. In her will, made soon after her marriage to Loye's brother George, she instructs her executors to repay the £80 to Loye. Elizabeth died in 1546 but at Loye's death in 1548 the debt had probably still not been repaid, as George at that time owed Loye £100. However, a bequest to George in Loye's will appears to largely cover the debt.

Loye left generous bequests to various relatives. George received his grey gelding, and George's second wife Jane his little white trotting nag and two gold rings, one with a sapphire. George, together with Loye's niece Katheryn Pylbarrow and cousins John and William Butler, also received an equal share of his plate, which included two gilt goblets and 12 silver spoons with the Ferrers arms. John Butler's wife was to have first choice. Loye seems to have taken a real interest in the welfare of Katheryn Pylbarrow. He left her £20 in trust with her brother Walter; there were strict conditions attached such that if Walter did not comply he would forfeit lands in St. Albans. He also left Katheryn £40. This again had an attached condition. In this case, if she was bullied and ordered in her marriage by the wish and counsel of his cousin John Butler, she would get 100 marks (£66 13s. 4d.). He also left her *"two fether beddes, two boulsters, two pillowes, two covletts and two trussing bedsteds"* to be delivered to her on the day of her marriage. As stated above it has not been possible to uncover the full details of Loye's close family, but Walter and Katheryn were most probably his sister's children. Similarly there is a lack of information regarding his relation to the Butlers. John and William Butler were the sons of Ralph Butler of Sawbridgeworth, Hertfordshire. Unfortunately, the surname of the second wife of Loye's father Thomas is a mystery, perhaps her maiden name was Margaret Butler. Alternatively, Loye's aunt Alice, the sister of Thomas, may have married a Butler. Whatever the relationship, two generations of his Butler cousins received legacies. John Butler inherited Loye's bay-fronted house; sadly the will does not tell us where the house was. There are also bequests to cousins with the surnames Hyde, Cartmells and Godyng and one of forty shillings to Lady Brokett.

The terracotta monument

It has long been assumed that the terracotta monument in one of the blocked arches on the south side of the chancel in the parish church of St. Mary the Virgin and St. Thomas of Canterbury, usually referred to as the Abbey, at Wymondham, is the tomb of Loye Ferrers. Francis Blomefield in his eighteenth century "Topographical history of the County of Norfolk" states that he *"lies buried under the old monument in the south wall, in the altar rails in Windham, but it hath no arms nor inscription."* However, terracotta monuments of this type only occur in England for a short period of time in the 1520s or early 1530s. In Norfolk other examples occur in St. George, Colegate, Norwich; St. Nicholas, Bracon Ash; and on a large scale in St. John the Evangelist, Oxborough. The Wymondham Bede Roll drawn up in 1524 records the blocking up of the two south arches; this seems to fit well

The terracotta monument in Wymondham Abbey

with the date for the terracotta. At that time the monks, as rectors of Wymondham, had rights to the chancel of the parish church. Importantly however, the date 1524 is most probably before Loye Ferrers transferred from St. Albans to Wymondham, and twenty-four years before his death. Here once again Loye's will is of value. In it he requests *"my bodye to be buried in Christian buriall according to the discresion of my executors."* If he was expecting to be buried beneath a pre-prepared monument at Wymondham he would certainly have indicated this in his will. It is likely, however, in the light of his association with Wymondham and the fact that he had been Abbot there, that his executors would have decided to have him buried there; especially as one of the executors, Thomas Essex, had been a fellow monk of Wymondham and was at that time a cleric at Great Yarmouth. Moreover, it is possible that he was buried in the chancel beneath (in front of?) the terracotta enclosed arch; thereby, creating the misapprehension that the terracotta is a monument to him. Unfortunately, as stated by Blomefield, no inscription or brass has survived, if one ever existed.

George Ferrers

Loye Ferrers' brother George became a prominent Tudor courtier to Henry VIII, Edward VI and Queen Mary until 1555, after which he largely disappears from public life. He held no appointments under Elizabeth I; probably as he is believed to have favoured Mary Queen of Scots accession to the throne, and may have been the author of an unpublished Latin work advocating her claim.

George was educated at Cambridge where he obtained the degree of Bachelor of Canon Law in 1531, and at Lincolns Inn until 1534. He is said to have had a reputation as an orator at the bar, but there is no evidence that he practised law. In 1541, he married Elizabeth the widow of Sir Humphrey Bourchier. At the Dissolution, Henry VIII sold to Sir Humphrey the monastery of Markyate in Hertfordshire, which he converted to a manor house. On his death Sir Humphrey still owed money to the Crown. Eventually in 1548, Edward VI granted the property to George; unfortunately Elizabeth did not live to see her husband take over the house, she had died two years earlier. George named the house Markyate Cell. The property remained in the hands of the Ferrers family for the next hundred years. In 1552, George was also granted the Manor of the neighbouring village of Flamstead. In 1538, along with forty-three others, including Walter Cromwell, Thomas Godolphin and Edmond Jermingham, he was appointed servant to Thomas Cromwell, Earl of Essex, Lord Chamberlain of England. From 1542 he was a page of the Chamber. He was a Member of Parliament for a number of constituencies:- Plymouth, 1542-45: Cirencester, 1547; Plymouth, 1553; Barnstaple, 1554; Brackley, 1554-55; and finally for his home town of St. Albans in 1571. Soon after becoming a Member of Parliament he was arrested on his way to the House of Commons for an unpaid debt of which he had stood surety. The result was a rather famous dispute as to the privileges of members of Parliament. The House of Commons demanded his release but the Sheriff of London refused. The Lords and the Judges became involved and George was freed. The Sheriff and his accuser, Mr. White, were both sent to the Tower and were only released after the payment of costs for the trouble they had caused. George is said to have served in the war against Scotland and France, but it is most likely that he just attended the King or the Duke of Somerset, the Lord Protector, in a civil capacity. He must have been well thought of by the King as in his will Henry left him 100 marks. At the court of Edward VI at Christmas 1551 and 1552 he was the Master of the King's pastimes. When, for the twelve days of Christmas 1553, the office of Lord of Misrule was revived he was chosen for the part. *"Garbed in a gorgeous costume of carnation satin striped with silver, he kept great state, having his own officers, including heralds, musicians and fools, some of whom were dressed as cardinals. The cost - over £300 - was astronomical, but the King loved it."* Outside the court he served as Justice of the Peace for Hertfordshire and Escheator of Bedfordshire, Buckinghamshire, Essex and Hertfordshire.

He was also a noted scholar, and is credited with having translated the Magna Carta and other medieval statutes. He was joint author with Baldwin of a collection of historical poems entitled "*Myrrowe for Magistrates.*" He most probably composed plays for the court 'pastimes' and the verses spoken by the Lady of the Lake at the Kenilworth pleasures in 1575 have been attributed to him.

George spent the latter part of his time with his third wife Margaret at his estate at Markyate. It is difficult to draw conclusions regarding a person's character from the limited historical snippets that are available from Tudor times, but two Star Chamber court cases indicate that he may have been rather intolerant. A tenant described him as "*a covetous man and ill to deal with.*" In 1562 following a riot in Flamstead, he was accused of packing a general sessions with his assured friends in the county. The other case involved the marriage of his stepdaughter, Elizabeth Preston to Thomas Searle a servant of the Earl of Leicester. He and his wife claimed that they had not consented to the marriage and that Rowland Carew, who had given away the bride, was not a relative. However, the marriage was declared legally binding as the contract had been signed in the presence of Mary and Jane Ferrers, George's daughters. George died in 1578 and was buried in Flamstead church.

The Wicked Lady of Markyate

Katherine the great-great-granddaughter of Loye Ferrers' brother George became the subject of a Hertfordshire legend. Katherine's father Sir Knighton Ferrers died within a year of his marriage and before Katherine's birth. Her mother remarried Sir Simon Fanshawe a Royalist widower of Ware Park. When the Parliamentary forces captured Ware, Katherine and her mother took refuge with Lady Bedell at Hamerton in Huntingdonshire. Katherine was the heir to the Manor of Flamstead. As soon as Katherine reached the legal age to marry, twelve, her stepfather sought to gain control of her estates by arranging her marriage to his son Thomas. John Laycock proved a willing priest and at age thirteen she was married to her stepbrother, Thomas Fanshawe, who was sixteen. After the death of her mother and their benefactor, Lady Bedell, Katherine aged eighteen and neglected by her husband returned to the family house of Markyate Cell. Thomas later succeeded his father as the 2nd Viscount Fanshawe of Dromore. Katherine never became Lady Fanshawe; she died aged only twenty-six in 1660, before her husband inherited his title and is buried at Ware, Hertfordshire. However, she did obtain notoriety as the legendary Wicked Lady of Markyate.

The Hertfordshire legend tells of Lady Katherine Ferrers of Markyate Cell, who was reputedly a notorious 'highwayman.' Although, at the time Katherine was plain Mrs. Fanshawe, it is certainly to her that the legend refers. How many of the exploits attributed to her are true is open to question.

The stretch of Watling Street in the neighbourhood of Markyate and Flamstead, Hertfordshire, was notorious at that time for highway robberies. Katherine was young, in her early twenties, and adventurous. The legend has it that she was influenced by her lover, Ralph Chaplin, a local farmer by day and a highwayman by night. How long they operated together is not known, but Chaplin was eventually caught and shot on Finchley Common while robbing a baggage waggon. It is after this that she is said to have terrorised the district at night dressed as a man and mounted on a fine horse. Her exploits continued for several years until finally when she held up a wagon on Normansland Common near Wheathampstead she met her match; having shot the driver, she was shot by one of two unseen passengers in the waggon. She managed to return home but, mortally wounded, died shortly after. She is said to have had a secret door to the house and a passage from her bedroom to the stables. Her ill-gotten gains were never found and are supposed to be buried under a tree by a well at Markyate Cell. There is a local traditional doggerel:-

"Near the Cell there is a Well,
Near the Well there is a Tree,
And 'neath the Tree the Treasure be."

Markyate Cell has suffered a number of fires and after the last of 1840, a concealed stairway was uncovered during the rebuilding. A highly fictional version of the legend was made into a film in 1945, starring Margaret Lockwood as the Wicked Lady.

With the death in 1660 of Katherine Fanshawe, the Wicked Lady of Markyate, the branch of the Ferrers family that included Loye Ferrers, the last Abbot of Wymondham, and stemmed from William Ferrers, 5th Baron Groby, in the 14th century, finally came to an end.

Bibliography

Baggs, A.P., *Sixteenth-century Terra-cotta Tombs in East Anglia.* The Archaeological Journal, vol. cxxv, 1969.

Bindoff, S.T., *History of Parliament. The House of Commons 1509-1558.* Secker & Warburg, London, 1982.

Blomefield, F., *A Topographical History of the County of Norfolk.* William Miller, London, 1806.

Burke, J., *Extinct & Dormant Peerage.* Colburn & Bently, London, 1831.

Burke, J.B., *Dictionary of the Landed Gentry.* Colburn, London, 1850.

Clutterbuck, R., *The History and Antiquities of the County of Hertford.* 1815.

Cussons, J.E., *History of Hertfordshire.* 1972.

Dugdale, W., *The Antiquities of Warwickshire.* 1656.

Emden, A.B., *A Biographical Register of the University of Oxford.* 1974

Foster, J., *Alumni Oxonienses 1500-1714.* Parker & Co., Oxford, 1891.

Gerish, W.B. *The "Wicked Lady Ferrers."* 1911.

Hasler, P.W., *History of the House of Commons. 1558-1603.* HMSO, 1981.

Johnston, W.M.(Ed.), *Encyclopedia of Monasticism.* Fitzroy Dearborn, Chicago & London, 2000.

Jones-Baker, D., *Tales of Old Hertfordshire.* Countryside Books, 1987.

Kett, L.M., *Ketts of Norfolk. A Yeoman Family.* Mitchel, Hughes & Clarke, 1921.

Martin-Jones, S., *Wymondham and Its Abbey.* Stone & Co., Wymondham, 1953.

Norris, H., *History of Baddesley Clinton.* 1895.

Weir, A., *Children of England. The Heirs of King Henry VIII.* Pimlico, 1977.

Calendar of Patent Rolls - Edward VI. HMSO.

Court of Request Proceedings. The Hertfordshire Genealogist.

Letters and Papers Foreign and Domestic - Henry VIII. HMSO.

The Victoria History of the Counties of England - Hertfordshire. 1971.

The Victoria History of the Counties of England - Norfolk. Constable, London, 1906.

Visitation of Hertfordshire, 1574 & 1634. The Harleian Society, London, 1886.

Elizabeth Ferrers, Will of. Prerogative Court of Canterbury 1547. PRO.

Loye Ferrers, Will of. Prerogative Court of Canterbury 1548. PRO.

Sir Edward Bensted, Will of. Prerogative Court of Canterbury 1519. PRO.

Thomas Ferrers, Will of. 1534. Hertfordshire Archives and Local Studies.

Acknowledgements

Thanks are due to the staff of Hertfordshire Archives and Local Studies; to Paul Cattermole, the Wymondham Abbey Archivist, for valuable discussions; and to Ann Hoare for the Wymondham Monastery drawing.